MATH ON
THE SUN

By Katherine Ponka

Gareth Stevens
PUBLISHING

Please visit our website, www.garethstevens.com. For a free color catalog of all our high-quality books, call toll free 1-800-542-2595 or fax 1-877-542-2596.

Library of Congress Cataloging-in-Publication Data

Names: Ponka, Katherine, author.
Title: Math on the sun / Katherine Ponka.
Description: New York : Gareth Stevens Publishing, [2017] | Series: Solve it!
  Math in space | Includes bibliographical references and index.
Identifiers: LCCN 2015051087 | ISBN 9781482449426 (pbk.) | ISBN 9781482449365 (library bound) | ISBN 9781482449631 (6 pack)
Subjects: LCSH: Sun–Juvenile literature. | Mathematics–Juvenile literature.
Classification: LCC QB521.5 .P66 2017 | DDC 523.7–dc23
LC record available at http://lccn.loc.gov/2015051087

First Edition

Published in 2017 by
Gareth Stevens Publishing
111 East 14th Street, Suite 349
New York, NY 10003

Designer: Laura Bowen
Editor: Therese Shea

Photo credits: Cover, p. 1 (sun) Aphelleon/Shutterstock.com; cover, p. 1 (metal banner) Eky Studio/Shutterstock.com; cover, pp. 1–24 (striped banner) M. Stasy/Shutterstock.com; cover, pp. 1–24 (stars) angelinast/Shutterstock.com; cover, pp. 1–24 (math pattern) Marina Sun/Shutterstock.com; pp. 4–24 (text box) Paper Street Design/Shutterstock.com; p. 5 Volodymyr Goinyk/Shutterstock.com; pp. 9, 19, 21 (partial eclipse) courtesy of NASA.com; p. 11 QuentinQuade/Wikimedia Commons; p. 13 Kelvingsong/Wikimedia Commons; p. 15 Christos Georghiou/Shutterstock.com; p. 17 Werieth/Wikimedia Commons; p. 21 (total eclipse) Naoyuki Noda/Taxi Japan/Getty Images; p. 21 (annular eclipse) Tomruen/Wikimedia Commons.

Printed in the United States of America

CPSIA compliance information: Batch #CS16GS: For further information contact Gareth Stevens, New York, New York at 1-800-542-2595.

CONTENTS

Words in the glossary appear in **bold** type the first time they are used in the text.

OUR STAR, THE SUN

When we look at the sky on a clear night, we usually see about 2,500 stars. However, there are more than 200 billion in our **galaxy**. There's one star we see during the day—the sun!

The sun is orbited, or circled, by eight planets, their moons, many asteroids, and everything else in our **solar system**. The sunlight that shines on Earth in just 1 hour could meet the world's **energy** needs for an entire year! In this book, you'll learn more about this amazing star we couldn't live without.

YOUR MISSION

You're the scientist now. You'll be using different kinds of math to learn about the sun as you travel there in the pages of this book. Look for the upside-down answers to check your work. Don't forget to send your **data** back to Earth!

This is how we see the sun from Earth. Earth is always traveling around the sun. One complete orbit is called a year.

5

SO MASSIVE

Earth is the third planet from the sun, but the sun is still so far away that it looks small. However, the sun is the largest object in the solar system. In fact, it contains about 99.8 percent of the solar system's total **mass**. If the sun were the size of a large beach ball, then Earth would be the size of a small pea!

YOUR MISSION

The diameter of a circle is a straight line from one side to the other side through the middle. The diameter of the sun is 865,374 miles. The diameter of Earth is 7,926 miles. How many more miles is the sun's diameter?

$$865,374 - 7,926 = ?$$

Mercury

Earth

Venus

Mars

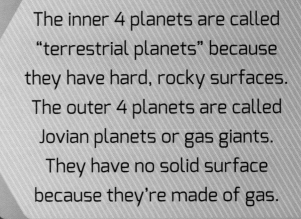

The inner 4 planets are called "terrestrial planets" because they have hard, rocky surfaces. The outer 4 planets are called Jovian planets or gas giants. They have no solid surface because they're made of gas.

Jupiter

sun

Saturn

Uranus

Neptune

ANSWER: The sun's diameter is 857,448 miles (1,379,929 km) more.

7

A FLAMING BALL OF GASES

The sun isn't solid. It's a flaming ball of gases that formed about 4.6 billion years ago. The gases are changed into energy at the sun's core, or center. The energy moves outward into the **atmosphere** and is then released, or let go, into the solar system as heat and light.

YOUR MISSION

Study the chart on page 9. Which 2 of the 10 elements listed make up most of the sun's mass? What is the total percentage of these 2 gases?

71.0 percent + 27.1 percent = ?

WHAT MAKES UP THE SUN?

ELEMENT	PERCENTAGE OF SUN'S MASS
hydrogen	71.0
helium	27.1
oxygen	0.97
carbon	0.4
nitrogen	0.096
silicon	0.099
magnesium	0.076
neon	0.058
iron	0.014
sulfur	0.040

This is a closeup photo of the sun's surface. Scientists think it takes about 170,000 years for the energy produced at the core of the sun to reach its outer zone.

ANSWER: Hydrogen and helium make up most of the sun's mass. The total percentage of the 2 gases is 98.1 percent.

THE SUN'S ROTATION

Like Earth, the sun rotates, or turns, on its **axis**. A spot anywhere on Earth goes around once about every 24 hours. However, because the sun is made up of gases, different parts rotate at different rates. A spot on the sun's **equator** takes about 25 Earth days to rotate. At its poles, the sun rotates once about every 35 Earth days.

YOUR MISSION

Scientists noticed the difference in the sun's rotation rates by observing dark areas called sunspots. Use the data above to find the difference between the rates of rotation at the sun's north pole and its equator.

35 − 25 = ?

The sun moves around its axis **counterclockwise**, as does Earth. The sun orbits the entire Milky Way galaxy once every 230 million years.

sun's orbit

ANSWER: There is a difference of about 10 days.

LAYERS OF THE SUN

The sun is made up of layers, or levels, of gas. The core is the hottest layer. It can be 27 million degrees F (15 million degrees C). The photosphere is the deepest layer that we can see. It can hit 10,000 degrees F (5,500 degrees C). The sun's outermost layer is the corona. It's as hot as 2 million degrees F (1 million degrees C) in some parts.

YOUR MISSION

Use the data above to place the 3 layers named—the core, the photosphere, and the corona—in order from coolest to hottest.

This is a picture of the layers of the sun according to NASA (National Aeronautics and Space Administration).

photosphere

inner core

radiative zone

convection zone

subsurface flows

chromosphere

corona

ANSWER: In order from coolest to hottest, the 3 layers named are the photosphere, the corona, and the core.

HOW FAR?

The planets have **elliptical**, rather than circular, orbits around the sun. That means their distance from the sun changes throughout the year. Scientists sometimes use a measurement called an astronomical unit (AU) to describe distances in our solar system. One AU is the average distance between Earth and the sun, or about 93 million miles (150 million km).

YOUR MISSION

Look at the graph on page 15. How many planets are more than 10 AUs from the sun? How many planets are fewer than 5 AUs from the sun?

Venus
Mercury
Mars
Earth
Jupiter
Saturn
Uranus
Neptune
sun

Neptune, the outermost planet, is about 2.8 billion miles (4.5 billion km) from the sun on average. That's about 30 times (or 30 AUs) farther than Earth!

AVERAGE DISTANCE OF PLANETS FROM THE SUN

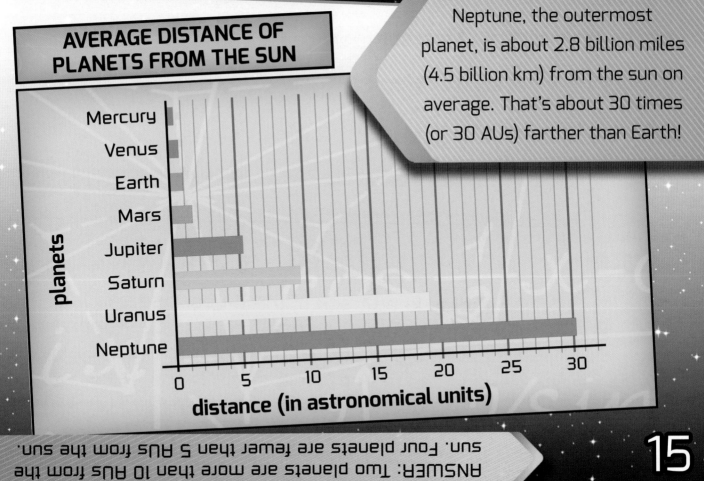

planets

Mercury
Venus
Earth
Mars
Jupiter
Saturn
Uranus
Neptune

0   5   10   15   20   25   30

distance (in astronomical units)

ANSWER: Two planets are more than 10 AUs from the sun. Four planets are fewer than 5 AUs from the sun.

15

SUNSPOTS

The magnetic storms on the surface of the sun are called sunspots. They look dark because they're cooler than the rest of the sun's surface. Most sunspots come and go in pairs or groups about every 11 years. Sunspots are usually found close to the sun's equator.

YOUR MISSION

Scientists keep track of the 11-year rise and fall of sunspots. They call it the solar cycle. A solar cycle began in 2008. What year is the cycle expected to end? About how many years would 4 solar cycles last?

$$2008 + 11 = ? \qquad 4 \times 11 = ?$$

The main parts of a sunspot are the umbra, or darkest part, and the penumbra, or lighter part.

ANSWER: The solar cycle is expected to end around 2019. Four solar cycles would last about 44 years.

GREAT GRAVITY

Gravity is the force that pulls objects toward each other. Earth's gravity is what pulls us to the ground and makes objects fall. The more mass an object has, the stronger the pull. The sun is much more massive than Earth—you could line up 109 Earths across the sun's diameter! So the sun's gravity is much stronger than Earth's.

YOUR MISSION

Since gravity is stronger on the sun, everything would weigh more there. A person who weighs 100 pounds on Earth would weigh 2,800 pounds on the sun. That's 28 times more than on Earth! How much would a dog that weighed 10 pounds on Earth weigh on the sun?

$$28 \times 10 = \text{?}$$

This image shows gas erupting, or bursting forth, from the sun. Earth is pictured to show you just how massive the sun is. You could fit 1,300,000 Earths inside the sun!

Earth to scale

ANSWER: The dog would weigh 280 pounds (127 kg) on the sun.

SOLAR ECLIPSES

A solar eclipse happens when the moon passes between Earth and the sun, blocking the sun's light. Partial solar eclipses cover part of our view of the sun, and total solar eclipses cover the whole view. An annular eclipse blocks all but the sun's outer ring. Solar eclipses have helped scientists study the sun's outer layers. What will we learn next about our amazing sun?

YOUR MISSION

Look at the chart on page 21. It tells when solar eclipses will occur and what kind they will be. What fraction of the solar eclipses will be partial?

$$\frac{\text{number of partial eclipses}}{\text{number of solar eclipses}} = \frac{?}{?}$$

SOLAR ECLIPSES, 2016–2019

September 1, 2016	annular
February 26, 2017	annular
August 21, 2017	total
February 15, 2018	partial
July 13, 2018	partial
August 11, 2018	partial
January 6, 2019	partial
July 2, 2019	total

People need to use special tools when watching solar eclipses to keep their eyes safe from the bright sun.

annular eclipse

total eclipse

partial eclipse

ANSWER: According to the chart, 4/8, or 1/2, of the solar eclipses will be partial.

GLOSSARY

atmosphere: the mixture of gases that surround a planet or star

axis: an imaginary straight line around which a planet, moon, or star turns

counterclockwise: in a direction opposite to the way the hands of a clock move

data: facts and figures

element: matter that is pure and has no other type of matter in it

elliptical: in the shape of an oval

energy: power

equator: an imaginary line around the sun, Earth, or other planet that is the same distance from the north and south poles

galaxy: a large group of stars, planets, gas, and dust that form a unit within the universe

mass: the amount of matter in something

solar system: the sun and all the space objects that orbit it, including the planets and their moons

FOR MORE INFORMATION

Books

Hunter, Nick. *The Sun.* Chicago, IL: Raintree, 2013.

Landau, Elaine. *The Sun.* New York, NY: Children's Press, 2008.

Owen, Ruth. *The Sun.* New York, NY: Windmill Books, 2014.

Websites

NASA: For Students
www.nasa.gov/audience/forstudents/k-4/
Learn more about outer space through activities, articles, and a picture dictionary.

Our Sun
www.kidsastronomy.com/our_sun.htm
Read the story of the sun, including how it formed.

INDEX